I MOVE
MOUNTAINS

I Move Mountains

Grief from the perspective of a
Christian man in the 21st Century

Thomas Henry Crisp

I Move Mountains

*Grief from the perspective of a
Christian man in the 21st Century.*

ISBN: 978-0-578-93219-4

I dedicate this book to all my friends and family who never stop believing in me or the God I serve. Walk the water. Climb the mountain.

Contents

Preface

I have had the privilege of witnessing Tommy Crisp's journey in life for much longer than the brief time period covered by this book. In my various roles as pastor, friend, and fellow worker in the kingdom of God, I have seen Tommy grow spiritually to the point where he was prepared to face the challenges recorded here, as well as to share the insights he gained from this experience. You can be confident that whatever he relates within these pages comes from a sincere heart that loves the Lord and wants to be a help to others who may be facing their own struggles in life. While you may find this singular event inspiring, what is even more uplifting is that it comes within the context of a life dedicated to bringing glory to God each day. Tommy continues to encourage those around him with his positive attitude, his dogged determination, and his steadfast faith even as his physical condition still seems to be deteriorating. I am often amazed at how he keeps going with the same spirit he exhibited as he faced the mountain and his monster as he writes about here.

If you know the same Lord whom Tommy knows, His presence, grace, and strength are available to you, too.

Whatever obstacles are in your pathway, whatever giants are ridiculing you, whatever challenges seem insurmountable, the same God who led Tommy will lead you. I pray that this story will inspire you in your circumstances to keep going, to tackle the impossible, and to trust the Lord to see you through whatever comes your way in life.

"Strengthen the weak hands, and make firm the feeble knees. Say to those who are fearful hearted, 'Be strong, do not fear!'" (Isaiah 35:3-4).

Tony Elder
Executive Director
National Association of Wesleyan Evangelicals

Acknowledgments

I am thankful for my wife, Heather. For almost three decades she has not only witnessed my struggles and victories, but she is a great supporter and encourager. It is a remarkable thing to be one with your bride. I would have been crushed if she told me, climbing the mountain is foolish. Instead, she knew, through God, all things are possible.

I am thankful for my brother, Eric. When I asked him to do this journey with me, without any hesitation, he said, "We'll get you up there." Eric boosted my confidence as I was at the beginning stages of training, struggling both physically and spiritually. I could not have asked for a better man to help me.

It is a blessing to have many brothers and sisters pray, encourage, and support this quest that God has sent me on. I have learned, many of my church family benefited greatly from watching and seeing my story.

God, who never gave up on me, who never left, and is always here. I want your people to see what I see. God, you gave me a gift I can never repay. The world has nothing to offer; no wealth, fame, drugs, or even a cure could replace this experience. Lord, you are beautiful. You mean everything to me.

A special thanks:

Rev. Tony Elder as theological advisor.

Moira McFarland for proofreading and advise on publishing.

MONSTER

"God may deliver you from the furnace, or He may walk into the fiery blaze with you. But one thing should be clear: You are not alone!"

Chapter One

Alone in a Crowd

Gravity always wins. As my knees hit the marble floor, the dull thud echoing down the hall, I can hear the gasps made by the people surrounding me. I hit so hard, my cane flies from my hand and bounces off the wall. On my hands and knees like some sort of four-legged animal, I can't decide what hurts more, my pride, my dignity, or my actual knees, which took the brunt of the fall. It doesn't matter, I suppose, since all three were bruised. As I look up, many sets of eyes are on me. One pair in particular stands out. A young lady whose face I'll never forget. She had this look in her eyes, a combination of concern and something I couldn't quite identify even though I saw it every time I looked in the mirror, and this is what finally broke my spirit. That someone could see what I saw. That someone else besides me was asking "why?" It wasn't the only question I had.

From Georgia to Michigan, I'd experienced MRIs, muscle and nerve biopsies, pokes and taps, and blood tests. I spent thousands of dollars just to hear a doctor call my case *interesting*. It sickens me that no one can tell me what is wrong with my legs. I'm losing strength daily and paralysis is setting in. I can barely make it into work. I am lost for direction. I have tried everything: medical doctors, physical therapy, and even homeopathic treatments. All are futile. "What am I going to do?"

Luckily, there is a metal rail within reach, and I grab it and lift myself up. I assure the onlookers that I'm okay and move forward, hobbling to the computer lab, carrying what I had left inside of me. What little bit there was, felt so heavy. I have all day to contemplate my emotions and what I need to "do." Men seem to gravitate on "doing." It seems that "doing" and "being" go together for us; you cannot have one without the other; do good, *you* are an angel; repair the car, *you* are a mechanic; invent a new medicine, *you* are a healer. "Doing" can be our downfall, but it can be our greatest attribute, too.

After work, I want to remain busy, try to keep my emotions in check. I start cutting the lawn. The grass needs to be mowed, and it is also something to "do."

Look at me, *I'm* a landscaper. Riding the mower keeps me busy but it's also cathartic. It's a perfect place for thinking, something I am trying to avoid so not to be faced once again with the question: "What am I going to do?" There are no real solutions, at least any I want. I know a wheelchair is in my near future, but does it have to be now? Being confined to a wheelchair brings its own problems, and as the caregiver said about my wife's grandmother, "Once they go in, they don't come out." It's not the end of life, but it sure is a radical change I want to avoid.

If you are a human, you are going to experience grief. Grief is the intense sorrow associated with the loss of something, and it comes in many different forms. You might experience grief if your car is stolen, or if you lose a loved one. Grief digs in deep when you finally realize the finality of the loss, and your life is changed because of it. We realize after much moaning and groaning that we are not in control of everything. I want to walk like a human being, she does not want to bury her baby, and he is looking for a real purpose. We can try to hold on to it, stop time, put it aside, but there is nowhere to grab. There is no metal rail you can reach for leverage. It is like trying to grab air. Life will keep going on with or without you.

As a teenager, I backpacked all over the Southeast, wrestled in high school, took my girlfriend to prom, and danced all the while, the **Monster** was just sleeping. There is nothing wrong with relishing the past, but I think one of the best things you can do in life is to make new memories. But when I think about my future, I'm met with more questions. As a man and husband, how am I going to be a protector and provider? What about my dreams? How will I not be a burden to my wife and family? It's more than worry and apprehension. It's the thought: Who am I now at this moment, and how am I going to cope with this reality?

However, you cannot live in the past or the imaginary future, you must live in the here and now. This is the place new experiences are made, where your family, friends, and neighbors help you form moments that build new memories. That is the problem with grief, it does not want you to. Grief has its agenda, to keep you where you are at, but you cannot stay there. Moving forward can be frightening, but you must face your fears. What is that fear? The fear of failing. The fear of the impossible. The fear that things cannot become better. The fear of losing your identity.

The good news is that you *are* in the present. The past is gone, and the future is not here yet. What you "do" *now* cannot affect the past, but it can shape the future. Though we can't change the past, we have a chance to change the future. And we don't have to do it alone.

He answered and said, "But I see four men unbound, walking in the midst of the fire, and they are not hurt; and the appearance of the fourth is like a son of the gods."

- Daniel 3:25

We all go through some sort of a tribulation; the Christian, non-believer, male, female, young, and old. No one asks for heartaches, grief, or stress. We want to avoid these things at all costs. As humans, we try to evade the unpleasurable, but it will find you sooner or later. How you deal with it makes the difference. Do not avoid the deep water (Psalm 69: 1-2). If you feel yourself sinking; dig deep in prayer Do not choke! You are wide awake, no longer on autopilot. Everything you do now has to be with intention. Every breath and stroke. The horrible experience you are going through now may be dark and seem like a curse, and you can try and deny its existence, but it's there. And I am telling you, Brethren, to face it. With one step of faith, you can enter the light.

For years, every morning, I say this simple prayer. It's small, yet so big. The prayer is, "Today Jesus, I am following you." That's it. Sounds simple enough, right? I am committing myself to Jesus every day when in joy, suffering, celebration, mourning, strength, and weakness. It's a constant reminder that Jesus is on the throne, despite my life's circumstances, and I must make a choice, to follow or not to follow our Lord. Jesus is with us, even when we are forced into the fiery furnace. There may be times when you do not "feel" His presence, but do not let that emotion cloud the fact that God is there. God may deliver you from the furnace, or He may walk into the fiery blaze with you. But one thing should be clear: You are not alone!

After cutting the grass, I sit on my porch with a glass of water to cool off. The yard looks good. I love the smell of cut grass. Everything is the way I want it: the grass is at the right height, leaves, and sticks mulched up, and the pretty birds can see all the worms. For this moment, life is perfect. However, that moment is always fleeting. Soon, the grass will need to be cut again, leaves and sticks will fall, and the birds will find another yard. It must be consistently maintained much like my sorrow, which is a **Monster**. It makes me outraged, crushing my serene moment of contemplation on the porch. Where should my sights be focused? Where are you, **Monster**? Come out and show yourself. I want to fight! I want to find that **Monster**, beat him into the ground, and break his neck. I am so upset. I kept telling myself to calm down. My wife Heather will be home soon, and I don't want her to see me like this. It would trouble her, but I'm so angry and so exhausted. I'm tired of everything. No one knows how I feel.

I tell myself the biggest lie, "I'm all alone."

Study Questions

Focus: Daniel 3:25 "He answered and said, "But I see four men unbound, walking in the midst of the fire, and they are not hurt; and the appearance of the fourth is like a son of the gods."

Read Hebrews 4:14-16 and Isaiah 41:8-10

What is or has given you the feeling of being alone?

Do these scriptures bring you comfort? Why?

Why do we as men think we have to *"do"* to fix our situations?

What is your Monster?

How do you feel about your Monster?

Share an event or a testimony in your life where God has shown up in a big way?

In your Christian walk have you ever felt invincible because you knew God was with you? Explain.

When do you feel most weak? Why do we have moments of doubt?

Do you relate to the faith of Shadrack, Meshack, and Abednego? Why or why not?

What would help build your faith?

Who in your brotherhood do you rely on for strength?

If you do not have someone you can confide in, seek them out. Ask one of the men from your church or a nearby fellowship. If you are alone and do not have a fellowship, pray for God to lead you to one.

Much like the lawn that needs to be constantly maintained, so does our faith. What are you doing to maintain your Faith? Are you:

- Refreshing the soul daily with God's Word (read Psalms 19:7-9)
- Reading God's word with INTENTION and PURPOSE
- Crying out to our Father God and telling him of your struggles and asking for strength, endurance, deliverance, or a miracle
- Sitting at the feet of Jesus in silence and listening (read Luke 10:38-42)

Prayer Request:

Lord,

Thank You for Your Word. Thank You for these stories
that remind us of Your greatness. Thank You for Jesus
our High Priest who is able to sympathize with us. Help
us to draw near to Your throne with boldness and
confidence, that we may receive mercy and find grace
in our time of need. May we be ever mindful of Your
Presence. In the name of Jesus Christ, our High Priest
we pray. Amen.

*Now may the Lord of peace himself give you peace at
all times in every way. The Lord be with you all.*

2 Thessalonians. 3:16

"The man could escape Bethesda, no longer with lost hope and broken dreams."

Chapter Two

I Remember Adell

Every study I have read dealing with men's issues, suggests men are in trouble. If you do not see that there is a War on Men, you have not been paying attention. Unfortunately, despite men's suffering, we hear Western society tell us, "Man up" or "Put your big boy pants on," without any care of what the root of their problems are. How does a man feel when his wife divorces him, taking the house, children, and part of his income? How does a young police officer, shot by a criminal, permanently disabling him, feel when he is no longer a major foundation for his family? All these things weigh heavily on the good man. Where does he go? How does he gain something he has lost? Do men sit down and share their feelings about these things? Sometimes, but overall, no, we do not do that! Most men do not like sharing their feelings. Ask almost any wife.

One of the things we go through when dealing with grief is loneliness. We tend to think that we must deal with a problem by our self and no one else is going to help solve it for us. Men shy away from asking for help. I don't think this is an ego problem, but it is part of our nature to be self-reliant. There are going to be times, too many to count, that we do need help. Even the Psalmist looked at the hills and asked, "Where does my help come from" (Psalms 121:1)? He knew it came from the Lord. Furthermore, loneliness seems to negatively affect our relationship with God. The Scriptures seem less vibrant, our prayer life weaker, and God's overall presence, a distant memory. However, we know those are just feelings and feelings do not always represent the truth. Just because you are in a troubling situation, and you have no idea how to get out of it, it does not mean God is not working on it or have a plan for you. God hears your cries and God is on your side. Let us be reminded, for the believer, God's love is everlasting, and He cares for you!

After this there was a feast of the Jews, and Jesus went up to Jerusalem. Now there is in Jerusalem by the Sheep Gate a pool, in Aramaic called Bethesda, which has five roofed colonnades. In these lay a multitude of invalids— blind, lame, and paralyzed. One man was there who had been an invalid for thirty-eight years. When Jesus saw him lying there and knew that he had already been there a long time, he said to him, "Do you want to be healed?" The sick man answered him, "Sir, I have no one to put me into the pool when the water is stirred up, and while I am going another steps down before me." Jesus said to him, "Get up, take up your bed, and walk." And at once the man was healed, and he took up his bed and walked. Now that day was the Sabbath. So the Jews said to the man who had been healed, "It is the Sabbath, and it is not lawful for you to take up your bed." But he answered them, "The man who healed me, that man said to me, 'Take up your bed, and walk.'"

- John 5:1-11

There were many sick people in this area, but Jesus turns his eyes to one man. He asks the man a question, "Do you want to be made well?" At first glance, this seems like an odd question. The man has been lame for 38 years. Of course he wants to be healed. Who wants to live on the ground? The life of being lame is hard: finding food, water, shelter, and dust is always in his nose. For sure, he wants to be healed.

Why did Jesus ask him that question? Perhaps the lame man had become complacent. What else does he know besides being a beggar? His life skills are laying on a mat. Furthermore, how long does hope last? How many times has he tried to get into the pool before he gave up and just settled for the state he was living in? Jesus had a reason for asking. Jesus does not want us to give up or give in. He wants to exchange our grief for joy, and believe me, it is a very good exchange rate. The Creator of the whole Universe is on our side. Do you think He just spun things into motion and walked away for us to be alone? Surely not!

The lame man answered Jesus saying, "Sir, I have no man to put me into the pool." This breaks my heart. The man wanted to be healed but had no one to help him. At some point, he realized, he could not do it by himself. This poor man had no one! Where will his help come from? It sounds like he has no wife, family, spiritual brother, or even a stranger to help him. He was alone to deal with his problem, a problem he would never

.ve himself. Who cares about the man who cannot do? Jesus simply says to him, "Get up, take up your bed, and walk." So, he did. No longer is he alone, no longer does he have to face life by himself. With Jesus, you can stand and walk, fully healed! I wish I could have been there, just to see the excitement in his eyes.

I love this account, but what does it mean for the man filled with grief and loneliness? Is this story alive in your heart? Does it give you real encouragement? Perhaps it does or maybe the grieving man needs to experience or see it for himself to know he is not alone. Let's be honest, sometimes we want to see it with our own eyes, to see God working miracles today. We can hear great testimonies of God's mighty works in people's lives and that can give us comfort. We might think, "If it happened to them, it can happen to me."

I Remember Adell

I remember you, Adell. I heard you sing in church and praise God with all your heart. I saw you love your husband; a good husband and father who took his family to church; a rock. I saw you love your children and the other children too; a mother to all living things. I heard you testify how great our God is and that He lives. I remember you, Adell.

I remember you Adell, when you got sick, I heard you sing in church and praise God with all your heart, even though you were weak. I saw you love your husband, knowing you were going to leave him behind. I saw you love your children and other children too, knowing you would not see them grow up. You testified how great God is and that He lives even though you were dying. I remember you, Adell.

When Adell was in hospice, I went to visit her. Like anyone, I wanted to express my sympathy and concern. I wanted to support and pray for her. To show her love. Just be a friend. If she needed comfort, I would comfort her. If she needed a hug, I would hug her. I sat next to her bed, and she gently took my hand. She had lost so much weight and her skin was yellow, but her smile was beautiful and her eyes full of love. She looked at me and said, "Tommy, I'm praying that God heals your legs."

I did not know what to say. With a limited amount of time left on Earth, she thought of me. It was all I could do to hold back the tears. I came to comfort her, instead, she comforted me. How can that be? That day, I saw a miracle, not in my legs, but in Adell and the God who lives inside of her. I will always remember Adell for the rest of my days.

Still on my porch and before taking my last sip of water, I look over at my little hobby shop behind the house and begin making plans. I need to do something. I decide on making birdhouses. Woodworking is physical, and it would be great therapy. I used to do quite a bit of woodworking but laid it down years ago because it had become too strenuous. Perhaps this is the challenge I need to force my legs to work.

Jesus not only healed the man but told him to take up his mat. Not only does this show us the full perfection of His miracles, but it says to me, the man could move on. The man could escape Bethesda, no longer with lost hope and broken dreams. I need that too. I need to escape my grief.

I saw a glimpse of God's glory; "Lord, show me more."

Study Questions

Focus: John 5:11 "…The man who healed me, that man said to me, 'Take up your bed, and walk.'"

Are you in need of healing? Why do you think Jesus asked what seems to be a silly question?

Just like the lame man, is Jesus calling you to action about a circumstance in your life? What specifically is He calling you to do?

Have you become complacent in your troubles?

Do you think God is active in your circumstances? Why or why not?

Are you being self-reliant about your circumstances or are you depending on God?

Read Psalm 121

Where does your help come from?

What do you think about God being constantly active in your life? In what ways do you see Him working?

Does it bring you comfort to know that God does not sleep or slumber? Why or why not?

Prayer Request:

Father,

Thank You for loving us and for being the Way. Help us as we struggle through this life. Be our constant reminder that You do not sleep or slumber. Help us to know that You are the source of all power and life. Encourage us in our walk, strengthen us though the challenges we face. In Jesus name, Amen.

And the peace of God, which surpasses all understanding, will guard your hearts and your minds in Christ Jesus.

Philippians 4:7

MONSTER

"A Christian brother is more than a friend. He is woven into you through Christ; not through DNA."

Chapter Three

All Suffer and Rejoice Together

The next day, at my little shop, I take a deep breath, bend over, and pull the garage door up. It's dark, but I can still see the mess. It looks like my brain feels: chaotic. I turn on the lights, which helps me to see even better how truly disorganized my shop is. I have a lot of work to do before I even hammer the first nail into a birdhouse. I must admit, I struggle. I am very thankful my wife helps me—not only physically, but also with my mental confusion as to where things are supposed to go.

Listen to your Christian brothers and sisters. They may see the light even though you may only see the darkness. Give them some credit. A Christian brother, for example, is more than a friend. He is woven into you through Christ; not through DNA. Just as you have a Heavenly Father that is his Father too. Both of you have been adopted into His family. A Christian brother is there for you day or night. Just pick up the phone. A brother is praying for you. Let him help you. We men need more interaction with other men. Together, we need to pray, study the Word, hold one another accountable, in unity. Never underestimate brotherhood!

The shop is ready. Everything is in its place. It's amazing how better we feel when things are where they should be. Chaos turns our life upside down. Just like my shop, life may at times be out of order. It's important that when we are waiting on God's direction, we keep busy in a positive way. Going back to the past will not solve our problems. My former life was full of sin. God made me into a new creation. He changed my life for the better. The old life leads to death and destruction. We must remember, God is not a fast-food joint where we can order and get what we want in a matter of minutes. However, I honestly believe, sometimes we are waiting on God to move while He is waiting on us. I need to hear from you, Lord.

Like me, my dad is a woodworker, and he invited me to his house for free wood. He has tons of it. He had several trees cut down on his property and took the logs to a local sawmill to be cut into planks. He told me he had more wood than he could use in a lifetime, and it was perfect for making birdhouses. Dad lives in the North

Georgia Mountains. It's beautiful there. His house is on the side of a mountain and has a spectacular view. This is where Dad retired, and if you ever visit, you will see why. It is the perfect place to get my mind in the right direction and spend some time with my Pop. How awesome is that? Even so, I keep waiting for the **Monster**.

I spent several days with Dad. I think he enjoyed spending time with me. My mom passed away from Alzheimer's last year, and he was still healing from the loss. I miss Mom, too. The wood was dry so all we had to do was run it through a thickness planer. The amount of dust and wood chips was unreal. These are good times! I felt like a kid again and I'm doing something. As a child, I had no worries. I had a Mom and Dad that took all those worries away. Skin a knee and mom would kiss it. Things like that! Do you ever wish you were a kid again? Do you ever look at your children and think about how lucky they are?

While at Dad's something kept distracting me, Pinnacle Knob, a splendorous mountain range you can see from his back porch. Dad describes it as "A lady laying on her side." You get the picture, right? Every so often while working on the lumber, I would find myself staring at Pinnacle Knob. Something mysterious was drawing my attention to it. I have too much work to do, I tell myself. I do not have time for sightseeing, look at me, "I'm a woodworker." Still, time and time again, I found myself just gazing up at the mountain. Is there something up there? Why am I so attracted to it? I've seen it a thousand times. What is the difference? I made a plan. Tomorrow morning, I would get up early, make coffee, go on the back porch, and stare aimlessly at the mountain until my curiosity was satisfied.

I woke up in time to view the sunrise over Pinnacle Knob. I sat in the chair with my hot cup of coffee watching God's creation come to life. Seeing the world wake up is a spectacular sight. As I focused on the mountain, my eyes were drawn to the top, to the flat rock formation. I imagine it presents a remarkable view for all those who are on it.

Dad woke up and joined me. I asked him if there was a road that led to the top. He said no, but he did know of a hiking trail. Do you think I could hike it? I'd like to see what's up there. I should have not asked him that question. I already knew the answer. With a sad look on his face, he informed me it was a difficult trail, steep and rocky. He must have hated to answer that senseless question.

It seems like the **Monster** is poking fun of me now. That's okay, poke fun all you want; I'm sitting here with Dad, drinking coffee. Like a bully, the **Monster** will not back down. He knew he could discourage me. He saw the sadness in my dad's eyes, and also in mine before I put my head down thinking the impossible. **Monsters** know these things. I still wish I could find this **Monster**. Messing with me is one thing, upsetting my dad is another. **Monsters** are nasty, filthy animals!

If one member suffers, all suffer together; if one member is honored, all rejoice together.

-    1 Corinthians 12:26

You are not alone in your suffering. People who love and care for you suffer too. Dad cannot take away my grief or heal my disease. It hurts him dearly. He has always attempted to hide the pain, but I know it is there.

"Dad, I want to build birdhouses."
"Tommy, come over and I'll help you."

Please remember, when we are grieving, we must never lash out at the ones who love and support. They too are suffering. Allow people to help you even when some help seems silly. This is not necessarily for your benefit, but theirs. The support they are giving you, no matter how relevant, helps relieve some of the pain they are feeling. Just as the eye is part of the body, so is the hand. Both need each other and both are part of the same body. Heather and I have been a part of and have led music ministry for 20 years. I used to think it was important that when in front of the congregation, I presented myself in a way that would not disrupt *their* worship. This included my suffering. I was wrong. You cannot fake real worship. Worship must be done in spirit and truth (John 4:23-24). During this time of hardship, I felt as though I was acting. I did this because I did not want to upset my brothers and sisters. How foolish of me. I should have said, "Guys, I am suffering. I'm still willing to lead but I need your prayers and help." And, when my suffering left, we could all rejoice together.

I have a shadow; the mountain is following me.

Study Questions

Focus: I Corinthians 12:26 "If one member suffers, all suffer together; if one member is honored, all rejoice together."

Read: I Corinthians 12:12-26

How does this scripture bring you comfort? Explain.

Why do you think men often find it hard to share their difficulties with one another?

When your mind becomes filled with chaos, do you look for wisdom in the body of Christ? Why or why not?

Why do you think God created the body of Christ to be one body but many parts?

How does this concept show us the need to be dependent on one another?

Do you generally depend on God or do you rely on your own abilities?

What do you think it means to be a weaker part? (v.22) Why are these parts indispensable?

Why is it easier to share victories than defeats?

By God's design we are commanded to do two things, what are they? (v.26)

What do you think it means to suffer with one another and to rejoice with one another?

Who are you suffering with today?

Who is suffering with you?

Prayer Request:

Father,

Thank You for Your divine design of the Body of Christ. Help us to build this brotherhood with Your love and kindness. Keep us ever mindful of the needs of our fellow brethren and keep them lifted before You in prayer.

Help those of us who are stronger to strength those who are weaker and those of us who are weaker help us to lean upon those who are stronger. Teach us about our part in the body of Christ, how we are to help one another physically and spiritually. Bless this fellowship and strengthen us in the power of Jesus Christ. Amen.

Finally, brothers, rejoice. Aim for restoration, comfort one another, agree with one another, live in peace; and the God of love and peace will be with you.

2 Corinthians 13:11

"My whole world is about to change, and I know it. Truth just captured my very existence, and I cannot reject it."

Chapter Four

Silence Is Not Always Golden

Home sweet home. Heather greets me with a smile and a kiss. She is impressed with the lumber I have stuffed into my Honda CRV. She is a little emotional too. She knows there is a battle raging and wants to support me. She has always given me support. I have an extraordinary, Godly wife who is always lifting me in prayer. Sally, my dear old beagle greets me too, wagging her tail and crying with excitement as to say, "Where have you been, I missed you?"

Despite our troubles, we should always take the time to think about the good things we have. When dealing with grief, we tend to ponder upon our bad situations. If we contemplate only that, flowers become ugly, celebrations will be sad and the whole world could burn, and we would care less. Our minds need to be renewed (Romans 12:2). I know how you might feel Brethren. We must ask, is that mindset God wants or, should our thoughts be honorable, just, pure, lovely, commendable, excellent and anything worthy of praise (Philippians 4:8)? Yes, it should! We know this, but how?

After dinner, Heather and I began to unload the lumber. I had built a lumber rack, but it is too small. Some pieces went on the floor. I broke the rule of, "The bottom shelf remains empty." That's okay, I'm going to plow through this wood.

The next day, I was ready to make some sawdust. My legs may be stiff and each step painful, but I am determined to stay busy while waiting for God's direction. I have to be careful; tools are dangerous, and I do not want to hurt myself. I pick out some lumber and begin to scribe the lines. It's funny how we like things straight and perfect. Nature is not like this. It has crooked branches and broken skylines. As children, we draw nature as we see it, but as we grow, we are taught to straighten things out: straighten your room, straighten your shirt, sit up straight, and finally, straighten up your life. Today, everything is expected to be straight, and this is where children have a great advantage.

I had a great start and feeling good about myself. Eventually, I'm covered with sawdust. Birdhouse parts are being stacked, and my legs feel less stiff. This calls for a celebration. I get a cup of coffee and sit to think a minute. My mind drifts back to Pinnacle Knob, the mountain. From that day forward, I keep thinking about it. It was as if I were back at Dad's house. It seems the mountain followed me home. Even in bed, while trying to sleep, the mountain evades my mind.

Expecting defeat, I didn't really think about attempting to climb it. I'm okay with that; I'm building birdhouses while waiting for God's direction. Besides, how could I climb it? My legs are so weak that if I fell, I would not be able to get up without assistance. I have muscles that no longer work and others that are completely gone. I wear a brace to keep my right ankle from folding over. I surrender! You win. Now, leave me alone. I pray several times, "God, please remove this mountain from my head, it's starting to hurt."

To the choirmaster. A Psalm of David. How long, O LORD? Will you forget me forever? How long will you hide your face from me? How long must I take counsel in my soul and have sorrow in my heart all the day? How long shall my enemy be exalted over me? Consider and answer me, O LORD my God; light up my eyes, lest I sleep the sleep of death, lest my enemy say, "I have prevailed over him," lest my foes rejoice because I am shaken. But I have trusted in your steadfast love; my heart shall rejoice in your salvation. I will sing to the LORD, because he has dealt bountifully with me.

-      Psalms 13:1-6

Does your situation make you feel like something you are not? We can try to reinvent ourselves, but I think, sometimes, we will end up like Frankenstein's abomination with pieces that do not belong to us. Grabbing an arm or foot, inserting a used eye, sewing it together only to make things worse. We try to fix a problem that is not ours to fix. Why? Many Brethren

53

have, at one point, felt abandoned by God, while knowing in His Word, it is not His nature to leave or forsake us, but our heart says otherwise. We are waiting, as if we were hanging on a cliff, hoping for rescue. How much longer? How much longer until my strength fades to nothing? I am unsure what hurts the most: the suffering or the silence. Panicking can set in, causing us to make bad decisions and attack God's character. No matter where we are in our relationship with Him, even in our darkest moments, God is willing and able to help us.

You might think there is silence, but when you come to a complete understanding of God's presence, the healing begins. God has never left. Where could you possibly go that God cannot (Psalm 139:7-12)? I know there are times when the light becomes dim, the goodness seems to fade away, and you just want to give up; Love does not want you to. When your hope shatters before your eyes, keep looking up and cry for mercy. The Father has much. My Heavenly Father has never let me go, He is faithful, and His love endures forever and ever. Amen

The next day I am searching for more lumber to cut out parts. I dig deep into the pile because the next birdhouse needs to be wide. The sun is blazing hot, and there is no shade. I don't care. I'm building birdhouses. Looking for the right board proved to be challenging as I had to move the smaller pieces out of the way to find the appropriate size. The noise I am making over-shadows the music from the radio.

In a small shop, things must be moved around continuously. Dropping lumber onto the floor makes an awful slapping sound. Almost anything you do makes noise. It just means you are doing something, and I was concentrating hard on getting this job done, so I could cut out more parts. With 3 boards set aside, I grab one and begin to drag it outside to my sawhorses for ripping.

Halfway outside, I heard a voice.

It was not audible, but it might as well have been. It scared me. My eyes water up and I stand there frozen unable to move or speak as if I had seen a ghost. Holding the board against my chest, my mind begins to race as I am trying to process what I had just heard. My whole world is about to change, and I know it. Truth just captured my very existence, and I cannot reject it. I know the journey God is sending me on. I know the direction and no longer feel lost. My prayer is answered. It will test everything; heart, soul, and mind. I feel a massive amount of joy, while being filled with wonder.

The Voice said, "I move mountains."

Study Questions

Focus: Psalm 13:6 "I will sing to the LORD, because he has dealt bountifully with me."

Read: Read Psalm 13

When we become overwhelmed in our circumstances, our minds become chaotic. We are unable to see things clearly or even see the truth. In these times we need to rely on God's truth, our past victories with the Lord, and our brothers in Christ.

What is a current or a past situation that had you asking the same questions King David asked the LORD?

How long Lord until You answer my prayer?

Have You forgotten that I am here?

Are You hiding from me?

How long do I have to put up with my own counsel?

How long will my enemies be exalted over me?

Do you think it is normal to have these questions?

What causes us to lose sight of the LORD?

In verses 1-4 King David is on the brink of death. He asked God to give light to his eyes lest he die. I am sure we have all been here at some point in our walk. Are you glad that David did not stop writing at verse 4? Look back at King David's response in verses 5 and 6. We will, from time to time, lose sight of the truth. Just like David needed to recalibrate his mind and heart, we will need to do the same. It is always those small words such as: **but**, **if** and **so**, that carry the most tremendous weight.

David said,

But I have **trusted** in Your *steadfast love*;

my heart shall **rejoice** in Your *salvation*.

I will **sing** to the LORD,

because He has *dealt bountifully with me*.

Don't listen to the enemy. He speaks half-truths and lies. He will tell you that the Lord has abandoned you and He does not hear you. **But,** look at what John saw and wrote for you.

Revelation 5:8 says,
"And when he had taken the scroll,
the four living creatures and the twenty-
four elders fell down before the Lamb, each
holding a harp, and golden bowls full of incense,
which are the prayers of the saints."

Take comfort in His Word. The Creator of the Universe keeps our prayers. Who can fathom?

Prayer Requests:

Father,

Thank You for the power of Your Word. Help us to mediate on Your steadfast love, Your salvation, the bountiful blessings You have bestowed upon us. Lord prepare our hearts for You to move our mountains. Strengthen us with Your Word. Give us a gentleness of spirit as we help our fellow brothers in their walk. Build up this body of believers, in the powerful name of Jesus we ask, Amen.

The Lord bless you and keep you; the Lord make his face to shine upon you and be gracious to you; the Lord lift up his countenance upon you and give you peace.

Numbers 6:24-26

"There is no mountain that God cannot move. Yet, what if I am the mountain? Indeed, I am the mountain."

Chapter Five

Small Seeds of Faith

Some Christians become fearful or cautious when another believer says, "God told me..." The doctrine of the Holy Spirit will be debated until our Lord returns. In respect of the Holy Spirit, I think A.W. Tozer says it best in his book, *How to Be Filled with the Holy Spirit*. He writes, "The Spirit of the living God brought an evidence that needed no logic; it went straight to the soul like a flash of silver light, like the direct plunge of a sharp spear in the heart." That is so powerful! The truth is: I was filled with fear. I did lose my identity. I was lost for direction. I lacked confidence. I needed more than, "It's going to be okay." I needed to hear it from authority, someone who knows me from the inside out. I needed to hear it from God.

Many times, when the Holy Spirt speaks to us, it is through His Word. In my very being, I heard the words, "I move mountains." I am thankful that we have the Holy Spirit that reminisces the words of Jesus (John 14:26) even when are thinking about something else. Something as simple as moving lumber. As I heard this, I thought of the words of Jesus.

> *Because of your little faith. For truly, I say to you, if you have faith like a grain of mustard seed, you will say to this mountain, 'Move from here to there,' and it will move, and nothing will be impossible for you.*

> \- Matthew 17:20

A mustard seed is tiny. My wife and I grow a deck garden almost every year. I always enjoy looking at the seeds. Seeds vary in size, color, and shape. It's the tiny ones you must show the most care. They easily vanish, sometimes becoming lost in the wind. Can we lose faith in the same way? Is our faith so tiny, it could slip out of our hand and fall under the deck, only to be lost? I lost faith in myself but not completely. I need to lose faith in myself. Think about this, moving a mountain is nothing for God to accomplish. There is no mountain that God cannot move. Yet, what if I am the mountain? Indeed, I am the mountain. Have I been too reliant on myself? It took several years to get where I am at physically. Over those years I went from walking, to using a cane, to crutches, and then a mobile scooter when needed. Each year, I lost the ability to do something but always managed to get by. I needed to completely lose faith in myself and rely on God. Letting go and giving it to God is easier said than done. However, that is the faith we need and it can be small like a mustard seed.

When we study history and the present day, we can see the accomplishments of mankind. From steam engines to the modern supersonic jets, humans have been and are still busy. In President John F. Kennedy's, Moon Speech, he said, "We choose to go to the moon. We choose to go to the moon in this decade and do the other things, not because they are easy, but because they are hard, because that goal will serve to organize and measure the best of our energies and skills, because that challenge is one that we are willing to accept, one we are unwilling to postpone, and one which we intend to win, and the others, too." Notice the word, "choose." He is saying, we are doing it because we can, and this is the choice we are making. And, we did go to the moon. However, self-determination and will-power will only get you so far. We went to the moon, but still have not cured the common cold. Does it simply mean we have not focused on a cure or is a cure out of our limitations?

In the way that God spoke to me, it made me feel like a new person. I felt the weight of the whole world lifted off my shoulders. The baggage I was carrying vanished. When I was in Boy Scouts, we played a trick on another boy. Yes, it was mean. We were on a backpacking trip and as we trekked, we would carefully put a small pebble in his bag; 1 became 2 and 2 became 4 and 4 became 8. After a few miles, the poor kid finally realized his backpack was too heavy. When he discovered the pebbles, he was mad and laughed at the same time. He took it well. Eventually our backpack can become too heavy. It can become so heavy that we are no longer able to carry it. We all have limitations.

I had to let go, stop relying on myself and rely on God. Just like a mustard seed, our faith does not have to be large. It simply means, we must have faith in God and not ourselves. I sensed God was about to take me on a trip of a lifetime. I guess some students require more lessons. I will be training to climb Pinnacle Knob. I do not know how this will be accomplished, but I knew this is the path God put me on, and I need to rely on Him to get there. No self-determination or will-power is going to get me to the summit; I only need to have a small amount of faith in Him. I am scared and excited at the same time. God, will I see you on top of the mountain? Are you there, waiting on me? Perhaps these questions will be answered.

When Heather comes home, I meet her at the car. I'm excited to tell her my experience. I say, "God moves mountains and I'm climbing Pinnacle Knob!" Her wide eyes look at me and she responds, "If you were anyone else, I'd laugh in your face. If God told you, you will do it." For the rest of the evening, we talk about climbing the mountain. We discuss diets and exercises for me to do while putting faith in God, that ultimately, it is He that will move me. We bow our heads and pray. I did not know it at the time, but for the next 6 months I would be at war. I've never been to war.

I choose to rely on God.

Study Questions

Focus: Matthew 17:20 "...Because of your little faith. For truly, I say to you, if you have faith like a grain of mustard seed, you will say to this mountain, 'Move from here to there,' and it will move, and nothing will be impossible for you."

Are you able to relate to Tommy?

What has you filled with fear?

Have you lost your identity (as a man, a husband, a father, a brother, a son of the Living God)?

Are you lost for direction?

Are you lacking confidence?

What do you need to hear from the Supreme Authority, the Living God?

Read: Matthew 17:14-21 and Mark 9:14-29 New King James

Both Matthew and Mark give an account of the healing of this son; however, they each have a different perspective. The Gospel of Mark gives a little more insight on the father's heart and tells of a special weapon.

What are the problems that Jesus identified in the disciples? (Matthew 17:20 and Mark 9:29)

Is your faith too small for the circumstances you are facing? Why?

Is it possible that the disciples were not focused on the power of God but their own inability?

What is the posture of the father? (Matthew 17:14, 15; Mark 9:23)

Are you kneeling before Jesus?

Are you pleading for His help?

Are you willing to take any help, even it is not what you have in mind?

What is the special weapon Jesus mentions? (Mark 9:29)

Why is prayer often our last resort?

Why do you think Jesus links fasting with prayer (*New King James*)?

Is fasting and prayer part of your life? Why or why not?

In both narratives Jesus commands, the father to bring his son to Him. What is Jesus asking you to bring to Him?

Prayer Request:

Father,

Teach us to view our circumstances from a spiritual perspective not from a carnal one. Help us to know our limitations and to know Your boundless power. If there is anything obstructing our belief or causing us to be stagnant remove it from us. Lord help us where we are lacking, help our unbelief. Thank You for equipping us with Your Word and the power of prayer and fasting. Teach us how to use these weapons. Help us to use them for the body of Christ and for Your glory. Constantly remind us of Your Supremacy. In the powerful name of Jesus, we pray, Amen.

"But you, Israel, my servant, Jacob, whom I have chosen, the offspring of Abraham, my friend; you whom I took from the ends of the earth, and called from its farthest corners, saying to you, "You are my servant, I have chosen you and not cast you off"; fear not, for I am with you; be not dismayed, for I am your God; I will strengthen you, I will help you, I will uphold you with my righteous right hand."

Isaiah 41:8-10

"Even as an introvert, I understand the power of a relationship."

Chapter Six

Two are Better than One

Crawl, walk, run, then crawl again. I do not know how long it has been since the treadmill was used last. It's in the spare bedroom, and I am going to use it to train. Before I start, I need music; something with a good beat and inspirational. Years ago, Heather and I had a mobile disc jockey company called Crisp Sound. We mostly did weddings. We had a great time doing it, and the small business provided extra money while I was attending college. After a few years, we decided to close the business, but I kept all the equipment. With large speakers and a professional amplifier to push the watts, the living room can wake the dead. First song, KB, a Christian hip hop/rapper; the whole house begins to shake as I turn it up louder and louder. Boom! Boom! I can feel the sound waves bounce off my chest.

I'm feeling pumped and ready to go! I look around for someone to high-five. No one. Just me and God and I dare not. But I can't help wonder if God has emotions too? I am full of excitement and certain He is, too. This is my first day of training. I have 6 months to lose 45lbs of fat and gain as much strength and stamina in my legs as possible. I adjust the treadmill to 1.3 mph and begin to walk. Immediately, the tightness in my legs shoots all the way to my lower back like a bullet ripping through muscle. Each step is very painful. Despite the pain, I have a part to do. In high school, my wrestling coach had a way of motivating us. At 5'5" and compact, he had the voice of a lion, "Let's go!" I'm moving further away from where I was. Has God put you on a direction that seems scarier than the path you were on? Brethren, I know how you feel. For sure, there are giants in the land (Number 13: 31-33), but remember, God is with you; trust in Him.

It did not take long before I was bent over on the treadmill, hanging on for dear life, while trying to pick my feet up. I keep thinking, "Just a little bit more," but that is it, I cannot go any farther. Drenched in sweat, I push the stop button and carefully sit in the chair beside me. I can feel my entire body shaking and it is not from the music. Sitting there, trying to catch my breath and slow down my heartbeat, I look up to see how far I have walked. This is not impressive! I was only able to walk 1/4 of a mile and I am spent. The rest of my day will be doing nothing but resting.

The next day I visit a chiropractor, Dr. David Pellington. The stiffness in my legs and back are too much to bear. Walking into his office, I notice he has displayed many beautiful paintings of nature on the wall. I see no straight lines. In the background, I can hear waterfalls, windchimes, and flutes. It is a very peaceful place to visit. He spends an hour stretching, twisting and massaging me. I am amazed at the results and ask about his teacher. He informs me that he has had many over the years. I tell him my testimony and that I am training to climb a mountain. He is very supportive of the idea and offers any assistance that I might need. There are some that cheer for the underdog and he is on my side. I am very grateful.

After 4 weeks of walking daily and revisiting the chiropractor, I make it to 3/4 of a mile and lose 15 lbs. Even though that is an accomplishment, I am nowhere close to where I need to be. However, I can now visualize the goal and I want desperately to share this journey with someone. In my heart, it has to be my brother Eric. I want someone I can fully trust. Someone who is honest with me. Sitting on the back porch I stare at his phone number. What if he thinks I'm foolish for wanting to take this challenge? He knows me well and has seen my legs deteriorate over the years. Eric does CrossFit and for his age, he is in excellent shape and health. He is also a fireman and medic. I'm very proud of him and the more I think about it, I can't ask for a better person to climb the mountain with me. I click his number and wait for it to ring.

Two are better than one, because they have a good reward for their toil.

- Ecclesiastes 4:9

I am an introvert. Meaning, I am okay with being alone, comfortable with my internal thoughts and feelings, or at best, working them out myself. I have often thought about driving out West, in the middle of the desert and staying there for a few weeks to enjoy nature and solitude. However, being an introvert comes with a cost. I must make a conscious effort to keep in touch with friends. It is not easy, but I love, care, and enjoy being with them. I hope I never offend them.

Solomon knew that two are better than one. I know within my whole being, I am going to make it to the top of the mountain. If I can no longer walk, I will crawl. It will not be a matter of "if." However, when on top, who will share the view with me? Who will give glory to God with me? Who will be there to witness a miracle? (2 Corinthians 3:5) That would be the reward.

I have no doubt the trail will be rough. It is reported to be covered with falling trees, big rocks and steep inclines. What if I fall and get hurt? Will there be obstacles that I am physically unable to manage by myself? I will be in the middle of nowhere, not on a treadmill in my home. If someone joins me, we can work together when it gets tough. If one of us falls, the other can lift him up. Even as an introvert, I understand the power of a relationship.

Eric answered his phone and I began to tell him the journey and quest that God is sending me on. After telling him, I asked, "Will you help me?" Without any hesitation, Eric said, "We'll get you up there." I am so moved and relieved to hear that. This encourages me greatly and gives me fortitude to carry on my training despite the physical pain it brings. For the next five mouths, I will be suffering daily to meet the expectation of obeying God.

I am thankful so many offered to help me climb the mountain.

Study Questions

Focus: Ecclesiastes 4:9 "Two are better than one…"

Read: 1 Samuel 18:1-4

What does it mean that Jonathan was knitted to David's soul?

Do you get the imagery of the Church being knitted and woven together?

How much do you love your own soul? How much do you love your brother's soul?

Are you knitted to your fellow Christian brothers?

Why do you think we were created to have companionship?

Can you remember what the first thing that God said was not good? (Gen 2:18)

Why do you think God created the Christian Brotherhood?

Read: Ecclesiastes 4:7- 12

In chapter 1, Alone in a Crowd, Tommy said, "I tell myself the biggest lie, "I'm all alone."

How is it possible to be surrounded by people and still feel alone?

What did King Solomon state about the condition of a person who is alone?

Tommy also spoke about being overwhelmed while looking at his woodshop. He needed someone's help to see beyond his chaos and help him get on track.

In verse 8, King Solomon talks about there being no end to the labor for a person who is alone.

How do you relate to this?

What situation has you overwhelmed with tasks that you are unable to do alone? (ex. mowing the lawn, organize your deceased loved one personal possessions)

What was the solution to Genesis 2:18?

Do you think the same sentiment applies for the Christian Brotherhood (that it is not good for us to be alone)?

Why do you think God designed us to need one another?

Why were we created with different gifts to strengthen and edify the body of believers?

Sometimes it not a physical need we have, sometimes it just having our brothers' strong shoulder and knowing with certainty that he will be there when we call. Do you agree?

Tommy told the story of him calling his brother and asking for his help. Eric gave Tommy words with certainty, "We'll get you up there!"

Are you too proud to ask for help?

Are you too weary to ask for help?

What words are you needing to hear with certainty?

Are you three cord strong while standing against the enemy or facing your struggles?

One on one you may fail, even two on one they may prevail, three on one surely your monster will flee.

Prayer Request

Father,

Your Word says how good and pleasant it is for brothers to dwell together. You have created us for companionship, You have created us to be a large body of enter woven believers called Your Church. Help strengthen us to be the Church You have called us to be. Deliver us from our blindness of not being able to see our fellow believers' troubles. Help us to be sensitive to the needs of others. Give us strength to ask for help when we need it and may we always find a strong shoulder to hold to in our times of trouble. Thank You for loving us enough to give us our Christian Brotherhood. In the All Powerful Name of Jesus, Amen!

May the God of endurance and encouragement grant you to live in such harmony with one another, in accord with Christ Jesus, that together you may with one voice glorify the God and Father of our Lord Jesus Christ.

Romans 15:5-6

MONSTER

"For all the critics, it's Peter's desire to go where Jesus goes. That means, even walking out on the rough and unpredictable sea."

Chapter Seven

Water Walking

I have 3 months to go before the start my journey up the mountain. I am only halfway through my training but will go whether I am ready or not. The date is set for March 17th. I am amazed where God has taken me. Even if I were to never step one foot on the mountain, the hints of God's glory that I have witnessed have given me new life. In so many ways, my soul has been satisfied, refreshed, and renewed, while knowing, God is not finished with me yet. So, I must press forward, obeying everything He asks of me. I must continue to put faith in Him and carry the cross daily (Luke 9:23) knowing, without any hesitation, I am nothing without Him, and He will see me through. The mountain is waiting.

I want to test myself. Near the house is a trail that is very popular for walkers, runners, and bicyclers. It is a beautiful, smooth, cemented trail that takes you away from the city noise and into nature. Heather comes with me. She drives my mobile scooter "just in case." This is a funny sight! I hear the buzzing sound of the scooter behind me. The scooter has been a lifesaver. We love camping and it has given me the freedom to explore wherever we are. Soon, I will be leaving the scooter behind, only trusting in God who has set me on this path of, "No Scooters Allowed." I am using a new set of crutches that are made in France. I don't know why this is funny to me, but it is. Never have I've owned anything made in France. How fancy is that? This is a good day, and my confidence is high.

My French crutches are working great as we reach the turnaround spot. I have walked one mile at this point without much effort. Sure, I'm slow but astounded I have made it this far. I went from barely walking into work to walking a full mile. We snap a few pictures and head back home. Along the way, many thoughts ran through my head; where I was and where I am going. With each victory, we must give glory to God. It does not matter how big or small the victories are. They are testimonies; not just for us, but for those who are watching and cheering us on. The glimpse of God that I see, others are seeing it too. Even the unbeliever may have to stand back and readjust their claims.

I do not give Satan any more credit than I must. He does not deserve it even though he has been an adversary from the beginning of time. The lines have been drawn and the war drums are sounding, and until Judgement comes, we are in this battle. For me and my family, we continue to stand with the God of peace (Romans 16:20). However, I still have a **Monster** to deal with. I have managed to keep him at bay, but occasionally, he pokes his head out. He's hungry. Even after walking 2 miles with the knowledge that God has gotten me this far, doubts and negative thoughts still enter my mind, and they feed the **Monster.** How weak am I?

On the outside, it appears that I am physically fighting, and yes, every day is a nightmare. The treadmill is like a torture device that I must force myself to use. After finishing my workout routines, I am left exhausted. However, it is the inside where the war is raging. Thoughts like: God, is this what you really want me to do? The mountain trail is steep, rocky, and full of ruts. How will this be possible? What if I fail; will it damage my faith? Will I chicken out? There is no way I can do this. It is too much and I'm too disabled.

Immediately he made the disciples get into the boat and go before him to the other side, while he dismissed the crowds. And after he had dismissed the crowds, he went up on the mountain by himself to pray. When evening came, he was there alone, but the boat by this time was a long way from the land, beaten by the waves, for the wind was against them. And in the fourth watch of the night he came to them, walking on the sea. But when the disciples saw him walking on the sea, they were terrified, and said, "It is a ghost!" and they cried out in fear. But immediately Jesus spoke to them, saying, "Take heart; it is I. Do not be afraid." And Peter answered him, "Lord, if it is you, command me to come to you on the water." He said, "Come." So Peter got out of the boat and walked on the water and came to Jesus. But when he saw the wind, he was afraid, and beginning to sink he cried out, "Lord, save me." Jesus immediately reached out his hand and took hold of him, saying to him, "O you of little faith, why did you doubt?"

-        Matthew 14:22-31

This is a very popular example of why we should always keep our eyes on Jesus. Peter's **Monster** was the storm. **Monsters** will try and drown you, while Jesus will keep you afloat. I have always found it annoying when Pastors only focus on Peter's failure. They seem to be very critical of Peter. I get it, Peter failed, and this is one of many times he fumbled. Let me ask anyone who has ever been critical of Peter: Have you even stepped out of the boat during a raging storm and walked on water? How many of us cower with storms all around us, even when Jesus is with us? Would stepping out of the boat be the last thing on your mind?

No one really knows why Peter asked Jesus to command him out on the water. Perhaps it was Peter's rash personality, or maybe it was Peter's great affection for his Lord. No matter what it was, Peter got out of the boat. I want to say that repeatedly. *Peter got out of the boat.* The very fact that you are out of the boat and walking on water is a miracle within itself. Look at you, walking on water. Keep going. Don't stop. Keep your eyes on Jesus and walk toward Him. For all the critics, it's Peter's desire to go where Jesus goes. That means, even walking out on the rough and unpredictable sea. How many times did the Disciples talk about Peter walking on water in the following years? Do you think they only focused on Peter sinking? I say not! Regret is a powerful thing that can haunt you for the rest of your life. Leave all excuses behind and go where He goes. Walk the water. Climb the mountain.

I found you **Monster!** You are in my head and you must leave. Go away! I know what you are **Monster**. You are me and I am the greatest obstacle to be closer to

God. You will not scare me into submission. Your ego will be crushed because I will only bow to my Lord. **Monster**, you gave it your best, but it is over. There is nothing left here for you. I am out of the boat, in the stormy sea, walking toward my Lord. My eyes are no longer focused on you **Monster**. You, **Monster** are a memory. Goodbye, **Monster**.

Everything is okay.

Study Questions

Focus: Matthew 14:27 "...Take heart; it is I. Do not be afraid."

Read: Matthew 14:22-33

Has Jesus ever shown up out of nowhere for you? If so, how did you respond?

Were you fearful?

Why do you think Peter said, "Lord, if it is You, command me to come to You on the water?"

Do you think it was for confirmation?

Do you ever hear Jesus speaking and need to confirm it is Him? Do you ever ask him for a confirmation?

Why did Peter begin to sink? (v30)

Do the storms around you ever draw your attention from Jesus?

Do you see this event as a failure for Peter or a huge leap of faith? Explain.

What do you think Peter learned from this moment?

What do you think the other Disciples learned from this experience?

Do you think the Disciples talk about Peter walking on water in the following years?

Do you think they only focused on Peter sinking?

How do you think Peter remembered this moment? Was it a failure? Was it a miracle? Was it a regret?

Do you relate more to Peter or to the other Disciples?

Have you ever stepped out in total faith?

Do you have the confidence to step out of the boat?

Is there a task, Christ is calling you to do at this moment in your life?

Are you needing some of Peter's boldness for the situation(s) you are facing?

Do you think the other disciples were ashamed that they did not have the courage?

Prayer Request:

Father,

Thank You for the encouragement and strength that Your word brings to our daily lives. Help us to know that You defy science. When man looks to science for knowledge and understanding, science is listening to Your command. Help us to not lose sight of You when we are in the storms of life, may we keep our focus on You. May we approach Your direction with certainty that you will walk us through. Give us a firm foundation to stand on even when we are seemingly drowning. Help us to be bold and to step out in faith for the task You have laid before us. Anoint us with the discernment. In Jesus name Amen.

And my God will supply every need of yours according to his riches in glory in Christ Jesus. To our God and Father be glory forever and ever. Amen.

Philippians 4:19-20

"We are quietly making our way to the top barely speaking a word to one another. This time, silence is golden."

Chapter Eight

For All Your Worth

The ascent. No one could wipe the smile off my face. Eric and I begin adjusting our backpacks and gazing at the trail ahead. This is it! I am about to climb the mountain. I feel strange, somewhere between reality and a dream yet wide awake. I cannot remember the last time I felt this happy. For the last 6 months, I have trained every day for this very moment. I would not be standing on the trail if it had not been for God. He has moved me this far, and He will move me the rest of the way. I once wondered and asked, God are you there? Will I see you on the mountain? However, I realize, thanks to Ralph Waldo Emerson, that it's not the destination; It's the journey. I also realized that God has been with me the whole time. We are going through this journey together.

My body is broken, I know this is true. Even with all the training, my legs are still weak and standing here makes them tired. God has not healed my legs, and I do not know if He ever will. It will always be an invitation. Over the course of time, I have taken what is left and strained to build up what I could. I lost 45lbs and can now walk 2 hours on the treadmill. God has made the impossible, possible. Over the months of training, I maxed out my condition, knowing it will not be enough. Standing at the bottom of the mountain, I must rely on God to manage the rest, to get me to the top. I have no choice, nor do I have worries; God has this.

Are not two sparrows sold for a penny? And not one of them will fall to the ground apart from your Father. But even the hairs of your head are all numbered. Fear not, therefore; you are of more value than many sparrows.

- Matthew 10:29-31

My war was never with my body, but instead, it was with my mind. My mind is fully healed. It's the one thing I least expected because I never knew I was the hideous monster. I am not the same person I was. The amount of garbage and rage stored inside is now empty and being filled with His goodness and mercy. I thought I was nothing, a person with diminishing value. I hated myself and who I turned into. I was tired of the constant disappointments of my life and became a person with no ambition. No one wants to look in the mirror and see that. Brethren, God loves you. When Jesus was on the cross, it was not just the pain and thirst He was thinking about, He was thinking of you. He was thinking of your worth!

My disability and grief no longer define me; God does, and He gives me purpose. While Jesus died for us, for the forgiveness of our sins, He also died so we can have a relationship with Him. I know the Creator, the Creator of me. He spent 6 months with me in a way that I cannot explain. It is truly beyond my simple vocabulary and understanding. There is no plan A or B, there is just His plan, and His plan is to put us back where we are supposed to be, a creation for His pleasure, and this gives me worth (Revelation 4:11). We are not an accident but part of a divine design. I am, because He is. He is the LORD! I am forever grateful.

The beginning of the trail is pleasant. It is surrounded with mountain laurel that almost covers the sky. It is March, and spring is fighting for its turn. Winter is still resisting. The surroundings have a rainforest feel with moss growing on the big boulders that stick out of the cliffs. I have forgotten how much I love backpacking.

Crossing over several tiny streams, I must be careful that I do not slip. An hour has passed, and I am feeling good. I am where I should be. I am answering the call.

Eric and I decide to take a small break and drink water. I am glad he is with me. He is trailblazing and turns around every now and then to check his brother. Eric is being very patient as I slowly take each step. He never says anything; just looks to make sure I am moving forward. It seems the tide has turned, and the little brother is looking out for his big brother. For some reason, he decides it's time to be silent and this will be his motive the whole way. Perhaps this is what I need. I think some people would be offended by this or find it strange. I think Eric wants me to work it out, knowing he is there if I need help. We are quietly making our way to the top barely speaking a word to one another. This time, silence is golden.

100

After 5 hours of hiking, I am becoming exhausted. I can barely pick up my feet and the rocks are purposely grabbing my toes, causing me to stumble. The trail has become a zigzag step to the top, surrounded with large pine trees instead of mountain laurel. I keep thinking we must be close, but the trail keeps going on and on. Over the last hour, I have been using my arms to compensate for my legs, and they are starting to fail now. I begin singing my favorite worship songs as an invitation for God's help.

Up ahead, a giant pine tree has fallen across the trail. I am tired and cannot imagine how I will navigate it. I need a break, so I take a seat next to the tree. My body feels like Jell-O, the kind that some of the older members of the congregation bring to the church supper. Still out of breath, I manage to tell Eric, "I'm so tired." He can see it. Eric looks up, noticing the trail ahead has more zigzags. He takes his backpack off and begins jogging up the mountain. He is so strong and fit compared to me. However, despite brokenness and weakness, we are made strong through Him (2 Corinthians 12:10). How strong, Brethren? Get up and walk!

A few minutes later, I can hear Eric saying, "It's not too much farther. You got this." I reach out my hand and he pulls me up to my feet. The broken silence becomes the vision of the finish line. I take a deep breath and begin to walk asking for the Lord's help. I am in a daze from exhaustion, but somehow, I am able to move up the trail. Everything is blurry, but I feel calm. Farther up the trail, I can see sunbeams through the trees. There's the summit. Emotions begin to stir inside of me the closer we get. I am almost there. Shadows are running away from the light.

Light always wins.

Study Questions

Focus: "When Jesus was on the cross, it was not just the pain and thirst He was thinking about, He was thinking of you. He was thinking of your worth!"

Feeling Unworthy – Being most worthy

Have you ever found yourself ready to embark on one of God's amazing quest? Explain.

What situations has God moved you in? Did you have the confidence that He will see you through?

Have you ever felt some of those emotions where you are a hideous monster, raging, nothingness, diminished value, a disappointment, no ambition? What made you feel this way?

Do you have a clear understanding who you are to God?

The enemy is good at waterboarding us with lies and half-truths of who we are. Sometimes we even do this to our own self. I hope that these scriptures will open our hearts and minds to how God views us. In the end, He is truly the only One who matters. Hallelujah!

God's truths will always remain, even when He spoke specific truths for a particular person or time. Know that His truth is the TRUTH, and we can delight in His Word.

1. God has chosen you to be His image bearer and ruler over His creation.

    Read Genesis 1:26-27

2. God chose you before the foundation of the world, blessed you and has adopted you.

    Read Ephesians 1: 3-10

3. God hand crafted you and knows you intimately.

    Read Psalms 139:13-18

    Read Jerimiah 1:5 (You may not have the gift of prophesy, but this scripture is still relevant for all believers)

4. God redeemed you with the costliest of payment.

    Read 1 Corinthians 6:20

    Read Deuteronomy 7:6

5. God created you with an eternal purpose.

    Read Ephesians 3:9-11

    Read Ecclesiastes 3:11

Did any of these scriptures refresh your soul?

If so, which ones and why?

Prayer Request:

Lord,

Thank You for Your Word which breathes life into dry bones. Help us to focus on Your truths. Remind us of these truths when we are in despair. Protect our hearts and mind from the enemy and even ourselves. May we always be reminded that we are part of Your Love Story. Thank You for your divine plan and Your persistent chase. In the Mighty Name of Jesus, we pray, Amen.

May the God of hope fill you with all joy and peace in **believing, so** that by the power of the Holy Spirit you may abound in hope.

Romans 15:13

"Some of the strongest Christians I know are the ones who have suffered the most. They have something many do not have: A living, breathing testimony."

Chapter Nine

Ugly to Beautiful

I find my second wind. At the top, the dirt path turns to granite. I am now standing on the rock. In front of me is a perfect ledge, a place to sit and take in the sight. There are mountains everywhere and I am above them all, closer to the clouds than I ever thought I'd be. This is a humbling experience, and it's all I can do to hold back the tears.

Eric asks, "You okay?"

I answer saying, "Yeah, I just can't believe it." I look over to my left in the direction of my dad's house. I can't see it from here, but I know it's there. Either way, I have a different point of view. A new perspective. Up here, things look smaller and the world is less relevant. Where I am right now, in this very moment, is the place I need to be and nothing else matters.

Not only that, but we rejoice in our sufferings, knowing that suffering produces endurance, and endurance produces character, and character produces hope, and hope does not put us to

shame, because God's love has been poured into
our hearts through the Holy Spirit who has been
given to us.

- Romans 5:3-5

Sometime in high school, I was diagnosed with an "unknown" neuropathy disease. That is the one thing that never changed, "unknown." It did not mean much to me at the time because I did everything I wanted. I was not disabled. The "unknown" had not ravaged my legs yet. However, my Mom felt differently and wanted me to talk to her pastor, Father Hanson. I was not a Christian at the time and did not think I would receive any benefit from him. Sure, I believed in God, and sure, there was a guy named Jesus who died on a cross, but so what? I agreed to talk to him even though I thought at the time that it was really Mom who needed the talk.

Father Hanson was a gentle soul and seemed to genuinely love people. He always had a big smile and when I think back, he gave wonderful hugs too. As he talked to me about my diagnosis, I sensed my future would be challenging. The doctor never said anything

111

about this. It was a real shocker! Someone had been holding back information. Was it the doctor, my mom, or both? Back then, Google did not exist for more information. Many questions popped in my head such as, should I be worried? Toward the end of our discussion, Father Hanson said, "God is going to use this for good." Then, he prayed over me.

I'll be honest, I did not want to hear that. It was like a father spanking his child and saying: This is going to hurt me more than you. It didn't make any sense to me. How is God going to use this for good? Besides, I don't want to be used. I didn't understand, and honestly, I didn't want to. I didn't want this new information to be true. However, as I learned decades later, no amount of avoidances will make something you don't want to hear, go away.

Paul, like Father Hanson, is telling us something we do not want to hear; to rejoice in our sufferings. We do not like that because we see no benefit from it. What good is there not to be able to walk? Who in their right mind wants to suffer, and how can you possibly rejoice in it? The truth is, we should not avoid suffering. God uses it to turn something ugly into something beautiful. This suffering you are going through, it may make you strong, humble, kind, patient, loving, forgiving, hopeful, and yes, joyful. Some of these attributes are missing in us.

Some of the strongest Christians I know are the ones who have suffered the most. They have something many do not have: A living, breathing testimony. They are true witnesses of the greatest expectation: hope. For the Christian, hope is more than a desire for a certain outcome. to happen. Hope for the Christian is God's love being poured into us through the Holy Spirit. This means Brethren, whatever tribulation you are going through, open wide so you can be showered with God's love and presence. If you want to truly experience this, prepare to rejoice in suffering.

Months ago, I was looking at the mountain from my Dad's house. Today, I am looking at my dad's house from the mountain. I now have a different perspective. God gave me a gift I can never repay. The world has nothing to offer; no wealth, fame, drugs or even a cure could replace this experience. With God, anything is possible.

I have 4 bars on my cellphone. I call Heather to let her know we made it. My lovely wife grew up as a tomboy. She played softball, rode dirt bikes, and has never been timid when doing *guy* stuff, while still being a lady. As soon as she answers the phone, I say, "I'm on top of the mountain." An uncontainable squeal comes from her voice. I was not expecting this. I think she's more excited than I am. She has many questions, but all I can say is, "It's beautiful." I have no other words to describe it. Before ending the call, I look up and the sky suddenly turns black. It looks almost wicked. Heather checks the radar and lets me know that a storm threatens. "I'll be praying for you," she tells me.

Dear Brothers in Christ,

We may have never met, but I want you to know I am thinking and praying for you. I see good men, like you, on bended knee every day. I see you across the street, building a house. I see you throwing a ball with you children. I see you working a second job to make ends meet. Your promise is a promise kept no matter what.

You are holding the door for the elderly and feeding the hungry. I see you standing up against injustice because you know what is right and true. Because of you, the weak do not need to be ashamed; your hands are strong, but gentle enough to hold a baby. Your words may be few, but your actions are mighty, and the world can never erase that.

When we come together in unity, I witness God reigning in your hearts. I am so proud and honored to be among you. You are more than a friend; you are my brother, and I will continually lift you up. Together, not only can we serve one another, but we can be a light to a world falling prey to darkness. Keep shining your light for all man to see.

Your Brother in Christ,
Tommy Crisp

Eric and I sleep through the night, undisturbed from nature's wrath. The next morning, unzipping the tent and poking my head out, I notice the ground is dry.

It seems the storm missed its target. That's okay, it will get another chance. For now, I am rejoicing and have another mission; to get off this mountain. Eric and I quickly pack up everything and head out. But, I want to look one more time at the view and let it burn into my mind the way light burns into the emulsion of film so that I never forget what God has done.

Lord, You're beautiful.

Study Questions

Focus: "God is going to use this for good."

Hope deferred makes the heart sick, but a desire fulfilled is a tree of life. Proverbs 13:12

Are you sick from a lack of hope?

When has this scripture been true for you?

When you think of hope, what definition comes to mind (a wishing well, crossing your fingers, a winning lottery ticket)?

Biblical hope is different from worldly hope. Biblical hope comes with a degree of anticipation, pleasure, expectation, and confidence of accomplishment.

Does this describe the hope you have in God currently?

Have you experienced biblical hope? If so, how has it been different for you than worldly hope?

Why are you cast down, O my soul, and why are you in turmoil within me? Hope in God; for I shall again praise him, my salvation and my God. Psalms 42:5-6a

Do the words of the Psalmist resonate with you? Why or why not?

Have you ever spoke God's truth to yourself? If so, when and what did you say?

Read Romans 5:1-5

Have you ever asked God, "What good is going to come of this situation?"

What are some situations where in hindsight you saw God mold your hope?

Do you know the peace that comes with this hope?

How is this hope generated?

Why do you think God uses this methodology to produce hope?

What are we to hope in (v2)?

What gives us the confidence of our hope (v5)?

It has been said that hope is faith in the future tense.

What does this mean?

How cheap would hope be or meaningless if it was without struggle?

Do feel that your struggles have increased your hope? Why or why not?

How is your faith today in relationship to your hope? Are they equal?

As, the Psalmist said, "HOPE in GOD", brothers! The hope that the world gives is false, weak, and ever failing. The hope that comes from God, will endure to the end. Hold on to His hope!

Prayer Request:

Lord,

What a privilege and honor it is to share Your story with my fellow brotherhood. Lead them and guide them in Your Truth and in Your Hope. Help them to understand what it means to have HOPE in the creator and sustainer of all things. Thank You for taking our ashes and turning us into to something beautiful that reflects Your image. Continue to hold us up when we are weak and help us to hold one another up when we are strong. Help us to know with all certainty that something good is coming. In the Most High Name of Jesus we pray, Amen!

Let us hold fast the confession of our hope without wavering, for he who promised is faithful. And let us consider how to stir up one another to love and good works, not neglecting to meet together, as is the habit of some, but encouraging one another, and all the more as you see the Day drawing near.

Hebrews 10:23-25

Notes

Notes

Notes

Made in the USA
Monee, IL
18 September 2021